MORE FROM A BOOK

Visit abookapart.com for our full list of titles.

Publisher: Jeffrey Zeldman
Designer: Jason Santa Maria
Editor-in-Chief: Katel LeDû
Managing Editor: Lisa Maria Martin
Technical Editor: Eric Portis
Copyeditor: Katel LeDû
Proofreader: Caren Litherland
Book Producer: Ron Bilodeau

ISBN: 978-1-937557-77-5

A Book Apart
New York, New York
http://abookapart.com

TABLE OF CONTENTS

To the members of the RICG.

FOREWORD

WE WORK IN A DIGITAL MEDIUM, but there's a *weight* to our work. Over the years, the screens we design for have gotten considerably sharper. But as the quality of those screens has increased, so too have the images we've served to them. And, as you'll see in the pages ahead, those images are one of the chief reasons our websites have ballooned in size. Our websites may be prettier, but they're far, far slower.

our responsive designs have long made fine use of *flexible images*—by slapping `img { max-width: 100%; }` into our stylesheets, we have images as flexible as the fluid grids in which they're placed. But simply resizing an image with CSS won't help users on high-resolution screens; and delivering a huge, crisp image won't help users on punishingly constrained data plans. If we want to reach more devices, more *people*, with our responsive designs, `img { max-width: 100%; }` is a start—but it isn't enough.

Thankfully, the the Responsive Issues Community Group (RICG) was formed to address that dilemma. Lead in part by Mat Marquis, author of the little book you're about to read, the RICG developed a responsive images *standard*—a standard that allows us to deliver the most appropriate images to our users, based on any number of criteria. In other words, our images can now be as responsive as our layouts.

Now, that standard can appear intimidating at first, filled with obtuse-looking markup patterns. But if you're searching for a guide, you couldn't have picked a better one than Mat Marquis. Mat was responsible for shepherding this nebulous "responsive images" idea through the specification process, and he understands it better than most. In the pages ahead, Mat will use his indefatigable humor and wit to break down even the thorniest topic. Thanks to Mat's words, you'll be slinging responsive images in no time.

I'm glad you're about to read this funny, insightful, *powerful* little book. And I bet your users will be, too.

—Ethan Marcotte

INTRODUCTION

THAT FACT THAT YOU'RE reading this tells me something about you. It tells me that you're different from the way I once was.

I've been doing this—making websites—for a little more than a decade now. I like to think I've grown up some during that time. I don't mind saying I took some things for granted early on.

I've been incredibly fortunate, that much I've always known—and I'd appreciate it if you'd knock on wood for me here, reader. I've received way more than my fair share of help from friends, family, and total strangers alike. I've had—and have—the benefit of immense privilege. I've always tried my damnedest not to take any of *that* for granted.

What I took for granted were the *mechanics* of this work—at least at the start. If I made an element show up in the right place, on the right page, in the right browsers—no small feat, oftentimes—then my work was done. I'd never dig deeper than that surface level. I didn't know what I didn't know: that making a `div` show up in roughly the same place as a square in a .psd was just the tip of the web-development iceberg.

Below the surface—that's where the *meaning* is. To build a page that can be easily parsed by assistive technologies is to contribute to a more inclusive web; to render a page more performantly is to broaden the web's reach. To think too shallowly about a project means nudging the larger web in the same direction: toward something meant not for all, but for some; toward something meant only for those who experience it the way *we* do.

But I don't think that's who *you* are. Not now—not today, as you read this. You're ready to dive headfirst into a book about a subject that's easy to take for granted: putting images on the web.

At the risk of spoilers: any ol' image format in an `img` tag styled with `max-width: 100%` will get the job done. If all you were after was a passing grade, you wouldn't need to read any further. It might not be fast, it might not be accessible—it might not even *work* in some browsing contexts, depending on a set of factors you'd never come to know. But the job would, technically, be done. "*D* is for *diploma*" was my constant refrain in high school.

I can tell, though: scraping by isn't enough for you. Maybe you've been at this long enough to gain a healthy respect for your element, long enough that you don't take a single CSS property or markup pattern as a given. Maybe you're just starting out, sharp-eyed and voracious, looking to learn all you can about the web's inner workings. Maybe you're somewhere in between, starting to wonder what details lie beneath the surface of your workplace and your medium, the web.

Regardless of where you are in your understanding of the web, you know you want to make it work *better*. You want to play a part in building something faster, more reliable, and more inclusive.

If you believe that anything worth doing is worth doing well—hell, maybe even worth overdoing a little—then I've written this book for you.

Making the case

Listen: images do *damage*. The median webpage's total transfer size is huge: 1.7 MB, as of May 2018. Images alone accounted for roughly half of that.

It's not hard to see how the trouble started. Ultra-high-resolution displays feel ubiquitous now—I'm using one to write this, and I have more than one on my person as we speak. With the advent of Retina displays came the need for Retina-ready image sources—and that was just the beginning. Retina on the iPhone 4 begat Retina HD on the iPhone 6-8, then *Super* Retina HD Display on the iPhone X, and—if the pattern holds—we can expect Super Retina HD Display 2 Turbo: Tournament Edition in the near future. Of course, not to be outdone, manufacturers of countless mobile devices have continually upped the resolution stakes with each new iteration, in the exact same way.

That means trouble, for us and for users. It's no secret that there's a direct relationship between a site's performance and a user's willingness to, well, *use* it. Putting a bandwidth-obliterating wall of images—no matter how nice they are—between your users and the thing they came to your site to do will absolutely drive them away. An experiment done by Etsy a few years back saw an increased bounce rate of 12 percent from users on mobile devices when they added just 160 KB of images to a page.

This isn't an isolated incident. Check out any of the statistics on wpostats.com, a site dedicated to collecting this data, and you'll see the same results: from a business-case standpoint, you can very literally draw a line between users' time and their attention.

Web development is a game of inches. A stray comma breaks a build; a missing semicolon prevents a page from rendering. There's a lot of resiliency built into the web platform, but, ultimately, it does what we developers tell it to do. In aggregate, the web isn't a terribly opinionated platform—it isn't hard to think of the technology itself as neutral.

But nothing is ever neutral where people are involved—not technology, and not the tiny, seemingly inconsequential development decisions we make during the course of an average, boring workday.

I can't speak for you, reader, but in my day-to-day browsing context, an extra 160 KB here and there doesn't even register. As developers, we tend to occupy a position of privilege when it comes to using the web we're building. As a matter of occupational necessity, we have fast computers, modern browsers, and bandwidth to burn. That browsing privilege, unexamined, will skew what we build; unquestioned, it will lead us to unconscious bias. And our biases can have very real costs for others.

As of this year, according to Pew Research Center, one in five Americans owns a smartphone, but doesn't have a home broadband connection—up from 13 percent in 2015, and 8 percent in 2013. Likewise, a full 31 percent of adults making less than $30,000 a year have access to a smartphone, but no broadband connections in their homes, up from 20 percent in 2015. And 39 percent of adults with a high school diploma or less—a demographic I am part of—have a smartphone, but no home broadband.

These are all users who only experience the web by way of metered connections. Even users with an "unlimited" mobile data plan will have their connection speed throttled beyond a certain cap.

To reduce the browsing experience for these users is to limit their options—on the web and in their daily lives:

Among Americans who have looked for work in the last two years, 79% utilized online resources in their most recent job search and 34% say these online resources were the most important tool available to them.

Very few of us are likely to have built a job-search website. But maybe we built the site a user visited the day before they lost their job, the one that drained their prepaid data plan. Maybe it was something that could be justified in an early meeting: it was a site about art, so users should expect heavy images. It was a shopping site, so we figured nobody would be using it on their phone. It was a site for games, a luxury—but maybe that user gave their phone to their kid because they needed a little peace and quiet on the day they lost their job—a little time to think about what to do next.

A study conducted by Ericsson (PDF) in early 2016 found that delays in loading a mobile website caused, on average, a 38 percent increase in heart rate, and an increased stress level roughly on par with watching a horror movie or answering math problems. Honestly, that sounds right to me—you'd be hard-pressed to find anyone in any browsing context who isn't frustrated by a seemingly never-ending loading spinner.

But I don't mind admitting, here, to having recently experienced a *uniquely* exasperating "loading" animation during the process of checking my bank account balance while standing in a supermarket checkout line. I ended up losing my race against the cashier—or at least, my phone did. I was fortunate enough to have a declined card not cost me much more than my pride (*itself* a cost I'm not willing to foist upon anyone in a vulnerable position). But for a family that has to make every last dollar count, an unexpected overdraft fee could cost them a meal as well.

Building performant websites is a vast and ever-evolving discipline, ranging from tasks as large as compiling a web server to as small as optimizing the contents of a stylesheet. But it isn't a stretch to say that, on any given project, optimizing image assets and their delivery may be the single largest performance optimization we can make. If you care about building a more performant web, images are the place to start.

IMAGE FORMATS
AND COMPRESSION

OVER THE COURSE OF THE NEXT FEW CHAPTERS, we're going to cover a surprising amount of ground. But before digging into responsive image use cases and syntaxes—before combing through the nuances of browsers' speculative preparsers and how requests for image sources are made—we have to start with a little groundwork.

Choosing the right image format is a topic I'm betting will be familiar to more than a few of you. It might be a bit of a refresher for some, but I won't mince words: getting this part right can be far more important than any flashy new "responsive image" technique. An image source that is only a few hundred kilobytes as a JPEG might be several megabytes as a PNG-24, without any discernable difference in quality to the end user.

In making decisions about formats, encodings, compression levels, and so on, we need to consider the contents of the image: is it a real-world photo or an illustration? We have to decide one level higher than JPEG versus PNG: we have to look at vector versus raster formats.

VECTOR FORMATS

When we talk about vector images on the web, we're talking about Scalable Vector Graphics (SVG). I don't mind admitting I was a little resistant to SVG at first, even as it was becoming more and more commonplace. SVGs are made of *math*—and that alone was enough to bias me against it conceptually. I lived and breathed raster, and "vector" conjured up images of ill-fated forays out of my Photoshop comfort zone and into the uncanny valley of Illustrator—where my muscle-memory for key commands was just wrong enough to be frustrating, and where there were no comforting little squares to zoom in on.

But upon opening an SVG in my code editor for the first time—by accident, knowing me—I was presented with something immediately recognizable and deeply comforting: *markup*.

```
<?xml version="1.0" encoding="utf-8"?>
<svg xmlns="http://www.w3.org/2000/svg" width="400"
  height="400">
```

FIG 1.1: These three shapes use the same SVG markup—but their fill colors are controlled through CSS, the same way we'd style any other element on the page.

```
<circle cx="100" cy="100" r="50" fill="red" />
</svg>
```

Granted, it isn't HTML markup—but it's close enough to make sense at a glance. Those of you who have been in the industry for a while might recognize it as our old friend XML.

For simple edits, like changing the opacity or color of an icon, we don't have to fire up Adobe Illustrator—we can make those changes in the SVG itself. We can style them and animate them with real CSS, both in the SVG file and from the page that contains them (**FIG 1.1**).

We can even add custom *scripting* to an SVG, in order to bake behaviors and interactions into the images themselves (**FIG 1.2**).

And as much as that might appeal to us as designers and developers, SVG is also an *incredibly* powerful format in terms of the end user experience. It is, by any practical measure, an image format built for the modern web.

The most critical difference between vector and raster formats is—as the SVG name implies—*scalability*. To oversimplify, SVG is a method of communicating a series of coordinates to a browser's rendering engine, a set of instructions for how shapes should be drawn. The task of connecting these points is left to the browser—so when that set of coordinates is scaled up or down, the lines and shapes connecting them are redrawn to scale (**FIG 1.3**).

Raster images are more fixed: pixel-by-pixel instructions for rendering, with no fill-in-the-blanks for the browser in between. When scaled up—well, odds are you've seen the results in the

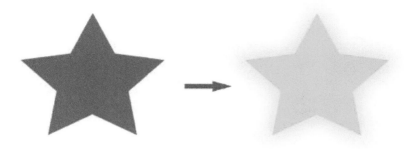

FIG 1.2: We can use JavaScript to add behaviors and interactions to an embedded SVG—such as toggling this star icon on and off with a click.

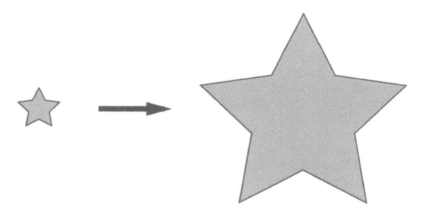

FIG 1.3: A resized vector image will be redrawn with sharp lines.

past, possibly by mistake. A raster image source scaled beyond its inherent dimensions tends to appear distorted, blocky, or blurred (**FIG 1.4**).

SVG doesn't suffer from this issue—a smooth curve between two points, drawn by the browser, will be redrawn just as smoothly at any size. We're going to spend a lot of time on the topic of ensuring that users receive viewport- and display-den-

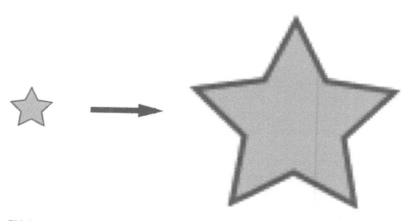

FIG 1.4: A raster image scales proportionally, and the result looks blurry at the edges.

sity-appropriate raster images—but with SVG, it's a given. And as you saw in the earlier example, the markup powering an infinitely scalable SVG source can be incredibly compact.

All that said, though, there are a few caveats to consider. Browser support for SVG is very good, but not guaranteed— not in the way that support for common raster formats can be universally assumed. Leaving a user without images in some contexts could very well mean leaving them with a website they can't navigate—so, depending on your project and how SVGs are being used, you might need to provide a fallback in the form of a better-supported raster version of the image source. All told, though, this is fairly easy to automate—projects like Grunticon handle generation of raster fallbacks for us, and there's a simple method for serving the correct asset to the end user. We'll talk more about that in the next chapter.

There's another catch with SVG, and this one is a key part of the decision between raster and vector for a given application: complexity. By nature of its function, the SVG format needs a little more active interpretation from the browser than raster formats—SVG's "draw a smooth curve connecting this point to that point" involves more thinking than raster's "draw a blue pixel, then a dark blue pixel, then a darker blue pixel, etc." For this reason, complex SVGs can be more taxing to render—and potentially larger, over-the-wire, than raster images.

There's no hard-and-fast rule there; it may take a little trial and error before you're able to instantly recognize an image source candidate as better served by SVG versus a conventional raster format. There are a few guidelines, though. For my money, I can say that interface elements—such as icons—are almost always better served by SVG than raster image sources. In fact, anywhere the icon fonts of yesteryear might have felt appropriate is likely to be a strong candidate for SVG.

For artwork containing multiple gradients, photo-realism, or intricate detail, though—when only pixel perfection will do—raster images are still the right tool for the job.

RASTER FORMATS

The lion's share of your content images—from photographs to animated GIFs—are going to be raster images. There's plenty more to discuss on this subject—and we will—but for now: think of a raster image as a two-dimensional grid made up of pixels, like so many brothers Mario.

When we break raster images down into formats—JPEG versus GIF versus PNG, and so on—what we're really talking about are the compression methods (or lack thereof) we're applying. Ultimately, choosing the appropriate raster-image format is about striking a balance between fidelity and file size.

Now, I'm the first to admit I don't have much of a mind for algorithms. But as a web developer—or maybe as the product of a Nintendo-centric childhood—I definitely have a mind for little pictures made of squares. So, in thinking about image formats, it helps to keep a pixel grid in mind (**FIG 1.5**).

Imagine this is the entirety of our source image. Choosing an image format effectively means choosing the method by which we're describing the contents of the file. For example, the top row of our grid could be described as:

- Row one, column one is blue.
- Row one, column two is blue.

FIG 1.5: Think of this as a close-up view of a raster image's pixels.

- Row one, column three is blue.
- Row one, column four is red.

But it could also be described as:

- Row one, columns one through three are blue.
- Row one, column four is red.

Assume you're playing the role of a web browser. You're ready—crayons and paper in hand—to render an image. I'm playing the role of a web server, and as such, I communicate in much the same way I do here in the text: I can't convey *an image*; I can only describe it.

If I were to ask you to draw a grid, and I read either of the previous descriptions to you, you'd end up with the same result—the same information is conveyed in either case. The first method does so absent any sort of compression: one "pixel" at a time. The second method, however, manages to describe the same image with far fewer characters. Or, in more practical terms: fewer bytes transferred over the wire, from the server (me) to the rendering engine (you).

Now, as you've probably guessed, this method of "encoding" and "decoding" an image doesn't resemble most actual formats in a meaningful way—there are often much more efficient ways to describe a grid, computationally speaking, than row-by-row and column-by-column. But it does come pretty close to describing one format: our old friend the GIF, animated or otherwise.

GIF

Saving an image as a GIF almost always means irrevocably reducing the fidelity of the original image. That might sound scary on the surface, but it's worth keeping in mind that our eyes, well, they don't have the best fidelity either. Fine-tuning image compression is about striking a balance between the level of detail we're able to perceive and the level of detail being passed along to the computer rendering that image.

Think back to our raster image grid, and how that information is passed from server to browser. This time around, let's add a little more detail: a single darker pixel (FIG 1.6).

As simple as this image is, it wouldn't take many characters to break this down into something human-readable:

- Row one, columns one through three are blue. Row one, column four is red.
- Row two, column one is blue. Row two, column two is dark blue. Row two, column three is blue. Row two, column four is red.
- Row three, columns one through three are blue. Row three, column four is red.
- Row four, columns one through three are blue. Row four, column four is red.

Assuming you and I have the same definition of "blue," "dark blue," and "red," that description would allow you to render a pixel-perfect interpretation of the original image. Think of this as a *lossless* method of compressing the image data for transfer from me to you. We've managed to condense the pixel-by-pixel description in a few places ("columns one through three are..."), but with no change to the visual fidelity.

Now, suppose we take a *lossy* approach to that description:

- Row one, columns one through three are blue. Row one, column four is red.
- Row two, columns one through three are blue. Row two, column four is red.
- Row three, columns one through three are blue. Row three, column four is red.
- Row four, columns one through three are blue. Row four, column four is red.

I've simplified the description of our original image, and the end result is that we've sacrificed pixel-perfection—as the rendering engine, you've rendered the image exactly as I've encoded it—but I left out the detail of the darker blue cell in my encoding, for the sake of a smaller transfer size. This specific lossy compression technique is called *quantization*, where a range of values are reduced to a smaller, approximated set of output values.

Reducing three colors to two across the span of a whopping twelve "pixels" makes for an obvious change (**FIG 1.7**). Across a larger and more detailed image, however, the effects might not be as noticeable—to a point. As we increase the lossyness of a GIF, the smooth gradients of the original image are replaced by a mottled effect (**FIG 1.8**). The file size plummets from around 318 KB to around 54 KB, and it—well—it becomes more pixel-y.

FIG 1.7: A lossy approach to compressing the previous image data means we've lost the dark blue detail.

We can reduce file sizes even further by manually restricting the color palette. What we end up with, then, is an image that retains the basic shape and hue of our original, but in a barely recognizable form (**FIG 1.9**). It would be smaller (weighing in at only 23 KB or so), but not terribly useful.

In practice, all of this means that GIFs are suited for a slim number of applications:

- limited color palettes and hard edges
- binary transparency (as in: a pixel is either 100 percent transparent, or 100 percent opaque)
- animation

All told, I don't find much call for an old-fashioned GIF in my day-to-day work, not anymore. Images with limited color palettes and hard edges—icons, line art, stylized flat-color illustrations—are almost always better served by SVG.

And I don't have much need for GIF-style binary transparency, either—not when PNG-24 handles transparency so much better.

As for animation, well...that's where I can't help but feel a little conflicted. I am, I don't mind admitting, something of an animated GIF enthusiast.

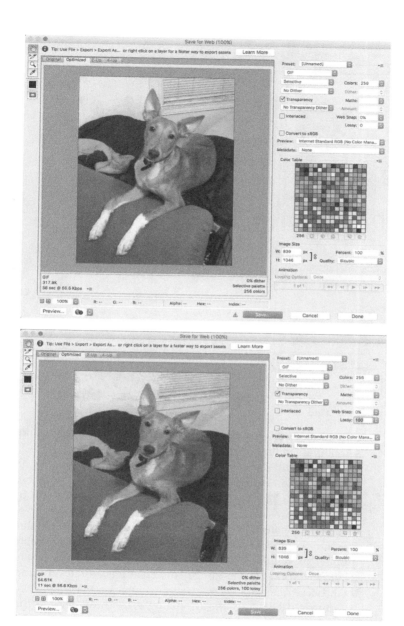

FIG 1.8: The more we increase the lossy compression, the more conspicuous it becomes.

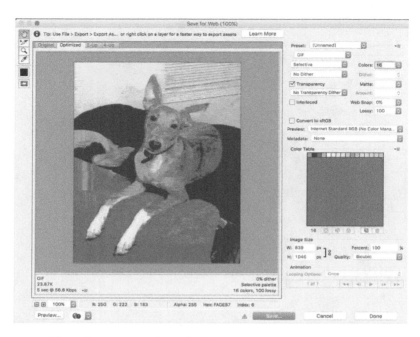

FIG 1.9: Taken to its extreme, we have a barely recognizable—if much smaller—image.

Animated GIF

For all intents and purposes, animated GIFs behave like self-contained flipbooks of individual GIF stills.

They're refreshingly simple, in both composition and use. If you see an animated GIF you like, you can grab it and throw it in a bukkit. You can open it up in an image editor, edit it, remix it, and resave it as a new GIF—Photoshop, for example, opens an animated GIF as a set of layers, each of which contains one frame of the animation. You can upload it to an incredible number of venues, with a click or a drag: chat clients, social media networks, text message conversations, whatever—and the process repeats.

Animated GIF *feels* almost analog, harkening back to the early days of the web itself—a little clunky, but made to be pulled apart and understood.

In every user-facing way, though, animated GIFs are practically indefensible.

They're slow to render, and excruciating in terms of file size. From an accessibility standpoint, it's difficult—at times, impossible—to sum up the contents of a complex animation in a single, terse `alt` attribute. The role of animated GIFs is almost invariably better served by short video clips—and video formats have the potential for richer accessibility features, like captioning and audio description tracks, more than an `alt` could ever hope to provide.

As such, animated GIFs are becoming less common. In fact, in order to retain the long-honed performance optimizations of the `img` element *and* make use of the reduced file sizes of video formats, several browsers have expanded the `img` element's `src` attribute to accept video source files—you can see this in Safari, at the time of writing, and Chrome isn't far behind. By any measurable metric, that's a win. Services like Twitter now convert animated GIF uploads to MP4 video, behind the scenes, before the associated tweet is posted, and that's a win too—it's great for performance and usability.

At my least generous, though, I can't help but notice that it provides Twitter with fertile new ground for advertisements. And those animations are now siloed—the generated files aren't something that a layperson can easily save, edit, or share on other services. Users can, of course, share a link to the tweet on Twitter dot com, and boost those engagement numbers.

Animated GIF—and maybe the GIF format itself—might just end up going the way of the carburetor and the record player. They're impractical, sure; nobody would argue that a record beats an MP3 for portability, or that an electronic fuel injection system is less reliable than a carburetor.

But still. There's just something warmer about analog.

PNG

PNG (Portable Network Graphics) comes in three variants:

- *grayscale* PNG, which is limited to black and white (or shades of gray)

- *indexed color* PNG (Photoshop calls it "PNG-8"), which can contain up to 256 colors
- *truecolor* PNG (a.k.a. "PNG-24"), which can contain many, many more colors—up to 16 million

There are a few things that set PNG apart from other formats. First, it was built for *lossless compression*, meaning that the encoding *itself* can be compressed—the way you might convert a huge text file to a ZIP to shave off a few bytes—but none of the actual image data will be reduced. In practical terms, that means that saving a source image as a lossless, truecolor PNG will never result in a drop in visual quality—but it *will* result in much larger files.

Second, while GIF handles transparency as sort of a binary proposition—either a pixel is 100 percent transparent or 100 percent opaque—PNG supports semi-transparency.

Between its large color palettes and its lossless compression methods, PNG-24 is a good choice for the canonical source version of an image—but rarely, if ever, the right choice. The use cases for PNG are similar to those of GIF: images with limited color palettes and sharp lines—cases where, more often than not, an SVG is the better choice.

You'll really only require a PNG when you need one specific feature: a raster-formatted image with transparency. Because PNG was designed to solve use cases that are now better served by SVG, you'll often see PNG used as the fallback version of UI elements in browsers that don't support SVG. Truth be told, that's almost the only time I use PNGs anymore.

JPEG

JPEG is far and away the most common image format used throughout the web, and with good reason: it's almost invariably the right choice for photographs. In fact, the use case is right there in the name, if a little obscured—"JPEG" itself stands for Joint Photographic Experts Group, the committee responsible for issuing the standard way back in 1992. You'll see the file extension for a JPEG as either .jpg or .jpeg, interchangeably.

JPEG is the poster format for lossy compression. Just like GIF, saving an image as JPEG means reducing the quality of that image. But unlike GIF, JPEG compression operates in a number of ways beyond quantization.

Let me get this out of the way right up front: unlike the refreshingly simple pixel-by-pixel encoding that GIF uses, JPEG compression is based on algorithms with names like "discrete cosine transform," which—to quote Wikipedia directly—"expresses a finite sequence of data points in terms of a sum of cosine functions oscillating at different frequencies."

Now, if this sentence has awakened in you a burning need to learn more about the dark and arcane math that powers images on the web, you have my blessing. However—and I cannot stress this enough—you *also* have my blessing to forget this information forever. Personally, I've never met an MIT URL that made a whole lot of sense to me.

So, in this section, I'm going to take a few liberties with the way a JPEG might be encoded into human-readable language. As you might expect from a format built around one computer communicating to another as efficiently as possible, it doesn't translate well to the written word.

Downsampling

Remember when I said our eyes are a little lossy in and of themselves? In terms of processing visual information, there's a lot we humans can't do very well. We're not great at processing "high-frequency detail"—we're able to recognize a tree, tell it apart from other trees, and even see a forest for said trees on a good day. But what we don't see—or we do *see*, I suppose, but don't fully *process* at a glance—are the positions of each leaf on the tree. We can seek out this information, for sure—but driving past a row of trees, we're not looking for each individual leaf in relation to those around them.

Likewise, come autumn, we see that the leaves on that tree have turned yellow—we can quickly absorb that there are different shades of yellow, the colors changing along gradients, the ambient lighting and shadow. We don't capture the precise hue of each individual leaf in comparison to the one beside it.

To put it in what I hope are increasingly familiar terms: we just don't have that kind of bandwidth. Mentally, we round things off, so we're not constantly overwhelmed by details.

JPEG compression attempts to compress an image source in a way that (loosely) matches the way our own psychovisual systems "compress" an image source. In effect, JPEG tries to throw away details we weren't likely to notice anyway so it can sneak the compression past us.

At its core, that isn't too different from a GIF; simply reducing the fidelity of a photograph ever so slightly might not register to our eyes, but it does reduce file size. With a GIF, removing a few colors from a photograph can mean a big reduction in quality for a relatively minor reduction in file size. With a JPEG, we can round down the level of detail in a way that might not register at all to our lossy eyes, if done within reason—*and* introduce far more opportunities for bandwidth savings.

JPEG does that rounding down—*downsampling*, it's called—in a particularly interesting way. It takes advantage of the fact that humans are more sensitive to differences in brightness than to differences in hue. As with GIF, color details (or *chroma*) can be reduced. Unlike with GIF, though, luminance details (or *luma*) are retained.

You can think of luma as a separate light/dark layer superimposed over our colors. For example, this photograph of a handsome dog—one who could *never* be mistaken for a deer—has been broken down into its luma and chroma layers (**FIG 1.10**). Superimpose those two layers again, and you have your source image (**FIG 1.11**).

It might seem like an academic distinction, as though GIF describes part of an image as "dark blue," while JPEG describes part of an image as "blue, dark." But by separating chroma and luma, JPEG is able to leverage one of our major psychovisual weaknesses: our eyes aren't as good at noticing slight differences in chroma as they are at noticing slight differences in luma. By throwing away detail from the layer we can't process as well but leaving the luma layer untouched, more opportunities for compression are created without causing noticeable degradation in the result. Slight differences in the *hue* of blue

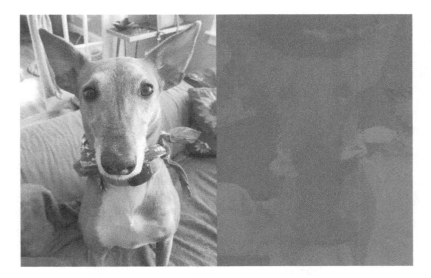

FIG 1.10: A photograph separated into luma (luminance) and chroma (color) layers.

FIG 1.11: While not explicitly encoded in the image, it can be assumed that the subject of the photograph is a very good boy.

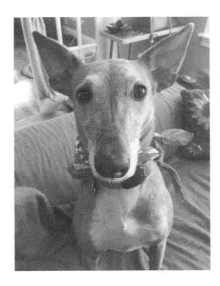

might be rounded down, but its brightness will be retained—and we likely won't notice.

Now, I mentioned before that JPEG has complicated, math-heavy methods of encoding images—we're not going to dig into those, but suffice to say that JPEG encoding doesn't encode images one pixel at a time the way GIF does. While "one pixel at a time, left to right, top to bottom" is easy for us humans to understand, it isn't a terribly efficient way to describe a source. So, instead, JPEG encodes the image as eight-by-eight blocks of pixels and describes the *blocks*—not the individual pixels inside them—algorithmically.

Consider that an image transfer is a computer communicating to another computer, and that sorting through information is something computers excel at doing efficiently, but in ways that aren't necessarily scrutable in writing. So, a grain of salt: I'm taking a few liberties as I convert aspects of JPEG encoding into human-readable language.

In terms of relayed instructions, you can think of JPEG downsampling as turning an image source into two sets of instructions. One encodes chroma:

- All blocks are blue.

The other encodes luma:

- The first half of the block at row two, column two is darker (**FIG 1.12**).

This may not seem like much of a win over GIF-style encoding, especially with this example—an image with flat colors and sharp lines. But JPEG is well suited to a much more common use case for images: gradients (**FIG 1.13**).

Describing a gradient using GIF-style encoding would be extremely verbose. Compressing it using GIF-style lossy compression would reduce the transfer size—but not without a pretty noticeable change in the rendered result. In restricting the color palette, we'd lose detail; the resulting image would have a sharp line between the light and dark shades of blue (**FIG 1.14**).

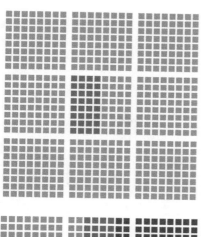

FIG 1.12: Rather than describing each individual pixel, JPEG encoding describes blocks of pixels.

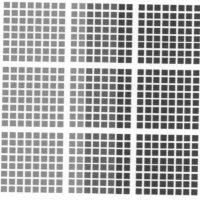

FIG 1.13: A pixel grid showing a light-to-dark-blue gradient.

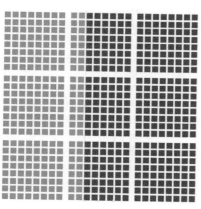

FIG 1.14: Our gradient pixel grid with GIF-style lossy compression applied.

FIG 1.15: An uncompressed image of the White Mountains in Vermont, weighing in at 1.54 MB.

A gradient isn't a strong use case for GIF, no matter how you look at it. But using JPEG's method of encoding our blue gradient source image would give us a very simple chroma:

- All blocks are blue.

It would yield a similarly terse luma:

- All blocks in column one are light.
- All blocks in column two follow a gradient from light to dark.
- All blocks in column three are dark.

Before we apply any compression, JPEG-style encoding gives us a small transfer for a pixel-perfect representation of our image source—so we know JPEG is the right choice.

Now, imagine this writ much, much larger—for example, with a photograph of the sky (**FIG 1.15**). GIF-style encoding barely halves the file size and creates perceptible stripes of blue across the sky (**FIG 1.16**). But with JPEG encoding, and a little quantization of the details—something our lossy psychovisual systems might not even recognize—the savings potential is huge (**FIG 1.17**).

FIG 1.16: Encoded as GIF and using a high level of compression, our file size is reduced to 38 KB, with a marked drop in quality. Notice the streaks across the sky, and the lack of detail in the foreground trees.

FIG 1.17: With moderate JPEG compression, the reduction in detail isn't apparent—and the file size is reduced all the way down to 26 KB.

Even if we only factored in this one approach to compression, you can see where JPEG is almost invariably the right choice for photographs: the real world is made up of gradients. You can likely also see where it isn't as well suited to the pixel-perfect use cases for GIF, like sharp text and hard lines—situations where pixel-perfection is necessary, even if it means sacrificing some algorithmic efficiency.

Artifacts

We could quite literally spend the remainder of this book going over JPEG alone. It would make for some dry reading, though, and steer us way into academic territory. I'd be remiss, however, if I didn't take a moment to mention the most infamous side effect of JPEG compression: artifacts.

You may not know them by name, but you almost certainly know them by appearance (FIG 1.18). JPEG *artifacts* result from JPEG compression taken to the extreme. Because JPEG compression samples and applies high-frequency detail-reduction in eight-by-eight pixel squares, we get—in strict technical terms—a blocky, glitchy version of our image.

Determining the ideal level of compression for your images is a finesse game, given the complexity involved in JPEG compression. When we're compressing images individually, we might be able to trust our gut—and our eyes. But summing up such a complex set of instructions with a single "quality" or "compression" number can be a fraught prospect. When it comes to setting sensible defaults—for example, automatically applying compression to user-uploaded images, the way WordPress does—what might work invisibly for one image *could* be noticeable in another.

There are tools that help remove some of the guesswork from the process—for instance, DSSIM allows us to introduce an intermediary step in our build or upload processes, analyzing each of our images for the optimal balance of perceptual fidelity and file size. That comes at the cost of higher processing overhead—paving the way for hyperoptimized content delivery services like Cloudinary.

FIG 1.18: A heavily compressed JPEG. The blurry, blocky, discolored effects are artifacts of the compression process.

But don't let that potential source of overhead discourage you. With a sensible default level of JPEG compression applied to all of our images, you and I might still be able to spot an artifact here and there. We know what we're looking for, after all, and we're focused on it—we're looking for the individual leaves on the tree, so to speak. But most users will just see a tree, with any faint artifacts blending in with the tiny details that their lossy psychovisual systems gloss over.

In fact, odds are you and I won't notice most of them either, even though we're wise to the tricks JPEG tries to play on us. For that reason, it's almost always a safe bet to nudge JPEG compression just a *little* lower than you think might be noticeable. You'll see it when you're looking for it, there in the JPEG compression options dialog, but when you're not—when *you're* the user—you'll likely fall for it, too.

Progressive JPEG

Progressive JPEG (PJPEG) effectively parallelizes the process of rendering a JPEG. Rather than the incremental rendering of a baseline JPEG (**FIG 1.19**), progressive JPEG breaks rendering into a set of full-sized "scans," with each scan increasing the quality of the image (**FIG 1.20**).

FIG 1.19: A baseline JPEG loads in gradually.

FIG 1.20: In modern browsers, PJPEG renders a low-quality version of an image first, then makes multiple passes at sharpening it.

The benefit is mostly perceptual. By delivering a full-size version of the image right away—albeit a blurry one—instead of empty space, PJPEG can *feel* faster to the end user.

That said, PJPEG isn't *strictly* a matter of user-facing smoke and mirrors. With the exception of *very* small image sources, PJPEG often means a smaller file size as well.

Browser support for rendering PJPEG isn't guaranteed, but it's very good. Worst-case scenario, the PJPEG renders all at once rather than, well, progressively. You'd lose the perceptual performance gains, but at no user-facing cost.

There is one trade-off: decoding PJPEG is more complex than plain ol' JPEG, and that means putting more strain on the browser—and a device's hardware—during rendering. That rendering overhead is difficult—but not impossible—to quantify in exact terms, but suffice to say that it likely won't be noticeable outside of severely underpowered devices. So, as in countless other web-development matters, I can't leave you with much more than a hearty "it depends"—but I will say I reach for PJPEG more often than not in my own work.

FORMATS OF THE FUTURE

Given that JPEG approaches compression in a handful of algorithmically intensive ways, you can probably see where there's nearly endless potential for improvement. The humble JPEG has given way to a number of slight variations, all of which aim to improve both image quality and transfer size by tweaking encoding and compression methods.

Once we start tinkering with encoding, however, there be dragons: even though some of these formats share the JPEG name, they're as fundamentally dissimilar as Java is to JavaScript. In order for those files to render, the browser has to be able to "speak" that new encoding. If we're not careful about how they're used, we run the risk of serving users an image file their browser can't render.

Some formats, like JPEG 2000—currently only supported in Safari—are intended to fulfill all of the same use cases as a baseline JPEG, but improve on the standard compression methods to deliver a visually similar but much smaller image. Other formats, like FLIF—not yet supported in any browser—aim to provide more efficient solutions to GIF-like animation and PNG-like transparency.

WebP is one of the more exciting formats, thanks in part to the level of interest it's seeing from browsers. This smaller, better-featured version of JPEG is currently only supported in Chrome and Opera, but Safari, Firefox, and Edge have all started experimenting with it as well—and, thanks to the responsive image patterns we'll discuss in the next chapter, we can use it responsibly right away.

RESPONSIVE
IMAGES

I COME HERE NOT TO BURY img, but to praise it.

Well, mostly.

Historically, I like img just fine. It's refreshingly uncomplicated, on the surface: it fires off a request for the file in its src attribute, renders the contents of that file, and provides assistive technologies with an alternative narration. It does so quickly, efficiently, and seamlessly. For most of the web's life, that's all img has ever had to do—and thanks to years and years of browsers competing on rendering performance, it keeps getting better at it.

But there's a fine line between "reliable" and "stubborn," and I've known img to come down on both sides of it.

Though I admit to inadvertently hedging my bets a *little* by contributing to the jQuery Mobile Project—a framework originally dedicated to helping produce "mobile sites"—I've always come down squarely in the responsive web design (RWD) camp. For me, the appeal of RWD wasn't in building a layout that adapted to any viewport—though I *do* still think that's pretty cool. The real appeal was in finding a technique that could adapt to the unknown-unknowns. RWD felt—and still feels—like a logical and ongoing extension of the web's strengths: resilience, flexibility, and unpredictability.

That said, I would like to call attention to one thing that m-dot sites (dedicated mobile versions of sites, usually found at a URL beginning with the letter *m* followed by a dot) did have over responsively designed websites, back in the day: specially tailored assets.

TAILORING ASSETS

In a responsive layout, just setting a max-width: 100% in your CSS ensures that your images will always *look* right—but it also means using image sources that are at least as large as the largest size at which they'll be displayed. If an image is meant to be displayed anywhere from 300 pixels wide to 2000 pixels wide, that same 2000-pixel-wide image is getting served up to users in all contexts. A user on a small, low-resolution display gets saddled with all of the bandwidth costs of massive, high-resolution images, but ends up with none of the benefits. A high-resolution image on a low-resolution display looks like any other low-resolution image; it just costs more to transfer and takes longer to appear. Even beyond optimization, it wasn't uncommon to show or hide entire blocks of content, depending on the current viewport size, during those early days of RWD. Though the practice became less common as we collectively got the hang of working responsively, img came with unique concerns when serving disparate content across breakpoints: our markup was likely to be parsed long before our CSS, so an img would have no way of knowing whether it would be displayed at the current viewport size. Even an img (or its container) set to display: none would trigger a request, by design. More bandwidth wasted, with no user-facing benefit.

Our earliest attempts

I am fortunate enough to have played a tiny part in the history of RWD, having worked alongside Filament Group and Ethan Marcotte on the *Boston Globe* website back in 2011.

It was, by any measure, a project with *weight*. The *Globe* website redesign gave us an opportunity to prove that responsive web design was not only a viable approach to development, but that it could scale beyond the "it might be fine for a personal blog" trope—it could work for a massive news organization's website. It's hard to imagine that idea has ever needed proving, looking back on it now, but this was a time when standalone m-dot sites were widely considered a best practice.

While working on the *Globe*, we tried developing a means of delivering larger images to devices with larger screens, beginning with the philosophy that the technique should err on the side of mobile: start with a mobile-sized and -formatted image, then swap that with a larger version depending on the user's screen size. This way, if anything should break down, we're still erring on the side of caution. A smaller—but still perfectly representative—image.

The key to this was getting the screen's width in JavaScript, in the head of the document, and relaying that information to the server in time to defer requests for images farther down the page. At the time, that JavaScript would be executed prior to any requests in body being made; we used that script to set a cookie about the user's viewport size, which would be carried along with those img requests on the same page load. A bit of server-side scripting would read the cookie and determine which asset to send in response.

It worked well, but it was squarely in the realm of "clever hack"—that parsing behavior wasn't explicitly defined in any specifications. And in the end, as even the cleverest hacks are wont to do, it broke.

Believe it or not, that was good news.

Prefetching—or "speculative preparsing"—is a huge part of what makes browsers feel fast: before we can even see the page, the browser starts requesting assets so they're closer to "ready" by the time the page appears. Around the time the *Globe*'s site launched, several major browsers made changes to the way they handled prefetching. Part of those changes meant that an image source might be requested before we had a chance to apply any of our custom logic.

Now, when browsers compete on performance, users win— those improvements to speculative preparsing were great news for performance, improving load times by as much as 20 percent. But there was a disconnect here—the *fastest* request is the one that never gets made. Good ol' reliable img was single-mindedly requesting the contents of its src faster than ever, but often the contents of those requests were inefficient from the outset, no matter how quickly the browser managed to request, parse, and render them—the assets were bigger than they'd ever need to be. The harm was being done over the wire.

So we set out to find a new hack. What followed was a sordid tale of noscript tags and dynamically injected base tags, of document.write and eval—of *rendering all of our page's markup in a* head *element, to break preparsing altogether*.

For some of you, the preceding lines will require no explanation, and for that you have my sincerest condolences. For everyone else: know that it was the stuff of scary developer campfire stories (or, I guess, scary GIF-of-a-campfire stories). Messy, hard-to-maintain hacks all the way down, relying entirely on undocumented, unreliable browser quirks.

Worse than those means, though, were the ends: none of it really *worked*. We were always left with compromises we'd be foisting on a whole swath of users—wasted requests for some, blurry images for others. It was a problem we simply couldn't solve with sufficiently clever JavaScript; even if we had been able to, it would've meant working *around* browser-level optimizations rather than taking advantage of them. We were trying to subvert browsers' improvements, rather than work with them. Nothing felt like the way forward.

We began hashing out ideas for a native solution: if HTML5 offered us a way to solve this, what would that way look like?

A native solution

What began in a shared text file eventually evolved into one of the first and largest of the W3C's Community Groups—places where developers could build consensus and offer feedback on evolving specifications. Under the banner of the "Responsive Images Community Group," we—well, at the risk of ruining the dramatic narrative, we argued on mailing lists.

One such email, from Bruce Lawson, proposed a markup pattern for delivering context-appropriate images that fell in line with the existing rich-media elements in HTML5—like the video tag—even borrowing the media attribute. He called it picture; image was already taken as an ancient alias of img, after all.

What made this proposal special was the way it used our reliable old friend img. Rather than a standalone element, picture came to exist as a wrapper—and a decision engine—for an inner img element:

```
<picture>
  <source …>
  <img src="source.jpg" alt="…">
</picture>
```

That img inside picture would give us an incredibly powerful fallback pattern—it wouldn't be the sort of standard where we have to wait for browser support to catch up before we could make use of it. Browsers that didn't understand picture and its source elements would ignore it and still render the inner img. Browsers that *did* understand picture could use criteria attached to source elements to tell the inner img which source file to request.

Most important of all, though, it meant we didn't have to recreate all of the features of img on a brand-new element: because picture didn't render anything in and of itself, we'd still be leaning on the performance and accessibility features of that img.

This made a lot of sense to us, so we took it to the Web Hypertext Application Technology Working Group (WHATWG), one of the two groups responsible for the ongoing development of HTML.

If you've been in the industry for a few years, this part of the story may sound a little familiar. Some of you may have caught whispers of a fight between the WHATWG's srcset and the picture element put forth by a scrappy band of web-standards rebels and their handsome, charismatic, and endlessly humble Chair. Some of you read the various calls to arms, or donated when we raised funds to hire Yoav Weiss to work full-time on native implementations. Some of you have RICG T-shirts, which—I don't mind saying—were *rad*.

A lot of dust needed to settle, and when it finally did, we found ourselves with more than just one new element; edge cases begat use cases, and we discovered that picture alone wouldn't be enough to suit all of the image needs of our increasingly complex responsive layouts. We got an entire suite of enhancements to the img element as well: native options for dealing with high-resolution displays, with the size of an image in a layout, with alternate image formats—things we had never been able to do natively, prior to that point.

THE FOUR USE CASES

Ultimately, those years of experimenting, prototyping, iterating, and arguing with each other impassioned discourse on various mailing lists gave us four mix-and-match use cases—four key problems with image delivery that any proposed solution (or solutions) *must* solve to be considered viable. In sum, the term "responsive images" refers to any combination of the following use cases:

- **Art direction:** requesting visually distinct source files at specific viewport sizes.
- **Image types:** requesting new image formats with responsible fallbacks.
- **Display density:** requesting image sources appropriate for high-density displays only when necessary.
- **Flexible images:** providing the browser with information about a set of image sources and how they'll be used in a page's layout, so it can make the most appropriate request for a user's browsing context.

Let's take a closer look at each of these use cases.

Art direction

The art-direction use case comes into play whenever

- you want to specify alternate versions of an image for different viewport sizes,
- you need explicit control over what sources appear when, or
- you need different cropping and zooming to best represent the subject of an image.

At any viewport size, the subjects of these images are the same—though their proportions may change across layout breakpoints (**FIG 2.1**). This sort of "cropping" can be achieved through CSS, certainly—but will still leave a user requesting hundreds of kilobytes of an image they might never end up seeing.

FIG 2.1: Different crops of the same image subjects are shown for different viewport sizes.

The markup for the `picture` element follows a precedent already set by HTML5's `audio` and `video` elements: a wrapper element containing `source` elements, each of which has an attribute defining the conditions for the use of that source (`media`) and the asset—or set of assets—to request if that condition is met (`srcset`):

```
<picture>
  <source media="(min-width: 800px)" srcset="pic-
  big.jpg">
  <source media="(min-width: 400px)" srcset="pic-
  med.jpg">
  <img src="small.jpg" alt="Cubes of tofu simmering
  in a fiery red sauce.">
</picture>
```

It's worth mentioning here that art direction does *not* apply to radically different image sources. A good rule of thumb is that you should be able to describe all of your sources with a single `alt` attribute—not least of all because you'll have to.

Similar to the pattern established by `video`, the `picture` element contains fallback content: an inner `img`. If the `picture` element isn't recognized by the user's browser, it's ignored. Its associated `source` elements are similarly discarded, since the browser doesn't have any context for them. That inner `img` element will be recognized, though—and rendered.

In addition to providing a robust built-in fallback pattern, `img` is the heart of the `picture` element in browsers that *do* support it. Rather than having `picture` recreate all of the accessibility features and performance optimizations of `img`—and adding a huge barrier to support for both browsers and assistive technologies alike—the `picture` element doesn't actually *render* anything on its own. Instead, it acts as a decision engine for the inner `img` element, telling it what to render.

The first `source` with a `media` attribute that matches the viewport size will be the one selected. There's precedent for this: the `video` element uses `source` elements, with `media` attributes, in the exact same way.

If we're using `min-width` media queries, we want to have our largest sources first, as illustrated in the example above. When we're using `max-width` media queries, we want to make sure our smallest sources come first:

```
<picture>
  <source media="(max-width: 400px)" srcset="pic-
  med.jpg">
  <source media="(max-width: 800px)" srcset="pic-
  big.jpg">
  <img src="small.jpg" alt="Cubes of tofu simmering
  in a fiery red sauce.">
</picture>
```

We'll *always* want to specify the inner `img` last in the source order—it serves as our default source if `picture` is unsupported, or if *none* of our `source` elements match their `media` attribute criteria.

Image types

The image types use case isn't concerned with viewport size or resolution—it's concerned with the image *formats* supported by the user's browser. It allows us to use the single-request fallback pattern already built into picture so we can serve alternate image formats in smarter ways.

One of the most common suggestions we'd hear from people just joining the responsive-images conversation was that we "just" needed a new format—a single image containing all of the different sources we could possibly need. The browser then would only request the appropriate part of that source file—and, in a vacuum, it's hard to argue with the logic.

But to make this happen, we would need to not only invent that new format, but also invent a reliable way to serve it to users with browsers that supported it, *and* invent a way for browsers to know which specific byte range of the file to load *without* requesting the entire "package" of images. The last bit would likely mean throwing together a new protocol for the web to run on. That was usually about the end of those threads.

It did get us thinking, though: one of the less impossible stumbling blocks to the introduction of any new format would be to serve it responsibly. A new image format can't have a fallback pattern in and of itself—if the browser doesn't recognize a file at all, it can't take advantage of a baked-in fallback pattern.

At the time, the best solutions all involved requesting and transferring the new image file *before* determining whether to throw it away and load a fallback:

```
<img src="image.svg"
 data-fallback="image.png"
 onerror="this.src=this.getAttribute('data-
 fallback'); this.onerror=null;"
 alt="…">
```

We were using this approach to contend with spotty browser support for SVG years before formats like WebP caught on. With this pattern, the request for image.svg would still be made in every browser. Once a browser had the file, it could figure out whether or not it was capable of *rendering* it. Browsers that couldn't render the SVG would throw an error. That error would trigger a line of JavaScript that did two things: first, it copied the contents of the data-fallback attribute into the src attribute, triggering a new request and rendering the PNG instead. Then, the script overwrote itself, to prevent any further errors from creating a loop if the fallback couldn't be rendered for any reason.

If it sounds a little convoluted, well, that's because it was— but when it came to making these decisions on the front end, approaches like this one were the only game in town.

But with picture, we were already inventing a decision engine—one explicitly designed to let us avoid redundant requests. Granted, that decision-making could never be completely automated—short of us *telling* the browser about a source file, there's no way for it to recognize a format it doesn't support without requesting it. We still need to provide the browser with information about the file so it can decide whether or not to make a request in the first place.

We can do that by using a type attribute on one of our source elements. In that attribute, we provide the *Media Type* (formerly MIME type) of the source. These can look a little arcane, but they all follow a predictable type/subtype format. For example, the Media Type for a PNG is image/png; for a WebP, it's image/webp.

With this syntax in place, we tell the browser to disregard a source *unless* it recognizes the contents of a type attribute:

```
<picture>
  <source type="image/webp" srcset="pic.webp">
  <img src="pic.png" alt="…">
</picture>
```

That code, for instance, ensures that any browser that supports WebP will get the WebP source, while every other browser will get the PNG (**FIG 2.2**).

One request; no wasted bandwidth. And this is forward-thinking: as newer and more efficient file formats come along, they'll come with Media Types of their own, and we'll be able to take advantage of them thanks to picture—no scripts, no server-side dependencies. Just good ol' img doing what it does best, with a little help from us.

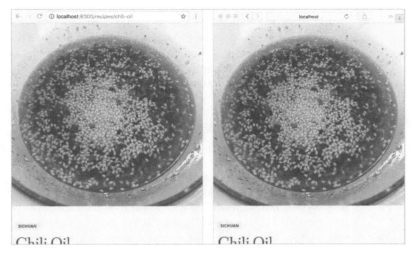

FIG 2.2: Users in Chrome (left) receive an 87 KB WebP, while users in Safari (right) receive a 132 KB JPEG.

Display density

The display density use case is about serving image sources that are appropriate to the hardware resolution of a device's screen—ensuring that only devices with high-resolution displays receive image sources large enough to look sharp, without passing that same bandwidth cost along to users with lower-resolution displays.

This determination hinges on a user's *device pixel ratio* (DPR). DPR is calculated by dividing a viewport's CSS pixels by the device's actual screen resolution, to get the number of real-world hardware pixels that make up a device's display.

For example, `@media(width: 320px)` will match on both an original, non-Retina iPhone and a Retina iPhone 5s—they both have a "normalized" viewport size of 320 × 568 CSS pixels. The actual resolution of the 5s *screen* is twice as high as that of the original iPhone, though: 640 × 1136. So, the original iPhone has a DPR of 1, while the Retina iPhone has a DPR of 2.

Likewise, the Samsung Galaxy S4 has a 1080 × 1920 display—but has a viewport of 360 × 640 CSS pixels. Because the Galaxy S4's actual resolution is three times higher than that of its resolution in CSS, it has a DPR of 3.

You can test this for yourself by opening the developer console of your browser and entering the following:

```
> window.devicePixelRatio
<- 2
```

In any browsing context, an `img` with a width of `100px` set via `width` attribute or CSS will occupy the same amount of the viewport—a normalized, CSS-pixel width of 100px. But in the devices with a DPR greater than 1, the rendered image has the potential to *look* sharper due to the resolution of the screen itself. In order to do so, the image being rendered has to have a natural width of at least 200 pixels. Once scaled down to fit in a 100-pixel space, that 200-pixel image source is rendered with double the pixel density. It won't look any different on a display with a DPR of 1, since that display can't make use of the increased density of the image. On a display with a DPR of 2, however, it'll look nice and sharp.

Once you've got the hang of DPR as a concept, the actual syntax that governs serving low-resolution versus high-resolution image sources is pretty straightforward:

```
<img src="sd.gif" srcset="hd.jpg 2x" alt="…">
```

This `x` syntax inside the `srcset` attribute acts as a suggestion to the browser, pointing out the source most appropriate to the real-world pixel density of the user's display. I say "suggestion" deliberately—but we'll get to that in a bit.

You'll notice that we also used this new attribute—`srcset`—inside the `picture` element, because this syntax can be used on those `source` elements as well:

```
<picture>
  <source media="(min-width: 60em)" srcset="big.jpg
  1x, big-hd.jpg 2x">
```

```
<source media="(min-width: 25em)" srcset="med.jpg
1x, med-hd.jpg 2x">
<img src="small.jpg" srcset="small-hd.jpg 2x"
alt="…">
</picture>
```

That's a *lot* of syntax, but before you panic: know that I've never actually needed to use this approach on a project. Not because there isn't an appeal to tailoring image assets to both viewport size *and* density—but because there's a much easier way. Weirder, maybe, but ultimately much easier: `sizes`.

Flexible images

So, we have a couple of options for explicit control over sources—and we'll need that sometimes, for sure. But in *most* cases, we want what we've always wanted in a responsive layout: an image that stretches to fit a viewport of any size, the way an `img` element with a single, gigantic source image would—we just want it to be more performant.

The flexible-images use case refers to these situations exactly—situations where we don't need explicit control over which source is shown when. The `sizes` syntax allows us to provide the browser with a couple of sources and some information about them, after which it completely takes the wheel and requests a single source. It's similar to the `type` attribute in that we're providing the browser with information about image sources up front, but different in that the browser uses a much fuzzier set of rules for determining what to do with that information.

Before we get into that syntax and how it works, a caveat: what we're going to cover here is a peek behind the curtain at the way the browser uses these attributes to make its decisions—it's not math you'll ever need to do. Fortunately, the *nature* of the math will be familiar to anyone working on a responsive layout: it ultimately comes down to "target divided by context," the same way we'd size an element in CSS.

But still, if you're as math-averse as I am, take heart: this syntax is strictly declarative. The `sizes` attribute is shorthand

FIG 2.3: These image sources are identical apart from their dimensions, which remain proportional.

for "here is the size of the rendered image in the layout," and the srcset attribute is shorthand for "here are the source files, and here are their inherent widths."

So, envision a 1600 × 1200-pixel image uploaded to a CMS, which then generates two more resized versions of that same image on the server: one that is 400 pixels wide, and another that is 800 pixels wide. These sources are identical in appearance, naturally, apart from their dimensions (FIG 2.3).

Pizza Dough

ACTIVE TIME: 30 min   TOTAL TIME: Overnight

Here at Wifно Makes Food Headquarters, we hold some pizza truths to be self-evident.

While not as good as good pizza, bad pizza is still pretty good. Pineapple is a viable—indeed, a desirable —topping. The "PIZZA TIME" pause music from Teenage Mutant Ninja Turtles II: Back to the Sewers won a certified banger. On these points—these incontrovertible truths—we can all surely agree.

Pizza time can, as we all know, strike without warning—it pays to be prepared. Throw this dough together, leave it in the fridge overnight, then chuck it into your freezer until such time as the urge for pizza strikes you. Be sure to give it enough time to thaw to room temperature first, plus a little time for the yeast to come out of dormancy and do its collective thing. You won't get much of a rise at that point, but y'know, we're not making deep-dish here. I make a fresh batch every couple times I feed my sourdough starter and store it gallon forever bag. A few hours before dinner, I grab it from the freezer, set it in a bowl of warm (not hot) water, and then—a quick shape and a little more rise time, and I'm good to go.

FIG 2.4: At this breakpoint, the largest space this image will ever need to occupy is roughly 25 percent of the viewport. Choosing an image source for this position based on viewport size alone would be tremendously wasteful.

The `sizes` attribute specifies the space the image will occupy in our layout—*not* the size of the user's viewport, as with media queries. After all, the size of the user's viewport doesn't really tell us anything about how an image is meant to be *displayed*, and that's how we want this decision to be made. Sizing an image meant to occupy 25 percent of a layout based on the width of the user's viewport would leave us with a much larger image source than the user will need (**FIG 2.4**).

Let's assume a fairly common instance: a "hero" image, up at the top of a page, occupying a space that spans the entire viewport (**FIG 2.5**). (It makes for easier math, for the sake of discussion.)

```
<img
  sizes="100vw"
  srcset="small.jpg 400w, medium.jpg 800w, large.jpg
  1600w"
  src="fallback.jpg"
  alt="…">
```

In this markup, we're saying *explicitly* that the space the image occupies in the layout has a width of `100vw`—100 percent of the viewport width.

FIG 2.5: The hero image for this recipe page occupies 100 percent of the viewport—so 100vw.

If we're looking at this markup on a device with a 320-pixel-wide viewport, 100 percent of that is, predictably enough, 320 pixels. That's our context. The browser takes that value—320px—and divides all the image-source sizes against it:

- Our smallest image has an inherent size of 400 pixels, so: 400 ÷ 320 = 1.25.
- Our medium image is 800 pixels wide: 800 ÷ 320 = 2.5.
- Our largest image is 1600 pixels wide: 1600 ÷ 320 = 5.

Those final calculations (1.25, 2.5, and 5) are, functionally-speaking, devicePixelRatio options—meaning that the browser is left with a set of source options that are *specific to the user's viewport size*. On a 320-pixel-wide viewport, sizes="100vw" is functionally equivalent to us writing out the following:

```
<img src="small.jpg 1.25x, medium.jpg 2.5x, large.
  jpg 5x" alt="…">
```

On a device with a devicePixelRatio of 2, the browser would likely choose medium.jpg—the closest match to 2x while erring on the side of not serving the user a blurry image. On a device with a `devicePixelRatio` of 1, the browser would likely serve us `small.jpg`.

If we were to visit a page using that same `sizes`/`srcset` syntax, with a viewport 640 pixels wide, the result of all that math would be completely different: `100vw` is now `640px`. When we divide our sources' widths against that, we get .625, 1.25, and 2.5. Those newly calculated values would be functionally equivalent to us writing this:

```
<img srcset="small.jpg .625x, medium.jpg 1.25x,
    large.jpg 2.5x" alt="…">
```

On a 640-pixel-wide viewport, our smallest image source will never match; that source is too small for any 640-pixel-wide viewport. Instead, `medium.jpg` will be chosen on `1x` devices, and `large.jpg` will match on `2x` devices.

If that all makes sense on your first read-through, you're in better shape than I was the first time I tried to make sense of it—and I helped write the spec. But it's important to keep in mind that we didn't have to think any of this math through when we wrote that markup: we only had to know our source files, their sizes, and the amount of space the image would occupy in the page.

You can probably already see where that adds up to a more common use case than the explicit breakpoints of `picture` when we're just looking to optimize requests.

Handling breakpoints

There's a little more potential for complication, even when we're just passing information along to the browser and letting it drive our responsive image decisions: a full-width hero image isn't the *least* common use of an `img`, but there's a much better chance that the space our image occupies in a layout is going to change across our layout's breakpoints.

In that case, we need to pass a little more detail along to the browser—and since the size of the image is going to change based on the media queries we're using in our CSS, we'll use media queries here as well.

YOSHOKU

Curry Rice

SERVES: 4   ACTIVE TIME: 1 1/2 hours   TOTAL TIME: 3 hours

For years now, I've been on a quest for the ultimate from-scratch curry rice recipe. No store-bought roux blocks; homemade stock, hand-toasted and ground spice blends. This is where I've landed thus far.

Recently popularized by coffee shop employment simulator Persona 5, Japanese curry rice (カレー, pronounced *karē*) is, in my opinion, the pinnacle of "fusion" cuisine: a Japanese dish, using French cooking techniques, based on Indian cuisine that arrived in Japan by way of England. What's really fascina—

Wait. no. shut up: why is there Marmite in this?

FIG 2.6: Our hero image occupies 100 percent of the available viewport width—until the viewport reaches 1200 pixels.

Let's imagine our hero image occupies 100 percent of the layout—but that layout has a `max-width` of `1200px` (**FIG 2.6**).

If we only used `sizes="100vw"` here, a user visiting the page with a 2000-pixel-wide viewport would get an image source appropriate for rendering *at* 2000 pixels wide. So, instead, we'll use `sizes` to tell the browser the following: on viewports up to 1200 pixels, this will occupy 100 percent of the viewport. On viewports at or above 1200 pixels, this image will occupy a space *exactly* 1200 pixels wide:

```
<img
  sizes="(min-width: 1200px) 1200px, 100vw"
  srcset="small.jpg 400w, medium.jpg 800w, large.jpg
  1600w, x-large.jpg 2400w"
  src="fallback.jpg"
  alt="…">
```

Let's break that value down step by step:

- (min-width: 1200px) we know well enough; in CSS, it means "the following applies on viewports wider than 1200 pixels," and that's what it means here.
- The 1200px that follows is the size of the space our image will occupy on viewports larger than 1200 pixles: 1200px of the viewport.
- The 100vw, preceded by a comma, isn't scoped to any media query—and again, just like styles in our CSS that aren't scoped to a media query, these apply unless that (min-width: 1200px) criteria is met.

Now, it's important to keep in mind that these values are *first match*—if (min-width: 1200px) doesn't match, the browser moves on to the next comma-separated value.

Let's add additional conditions to our sizes attribute above and step through them the way a browser would:

```
sizes="(min-width: 1200px) 1200px, (min-width:
800px) 80vw, 100vw"
```

- For a 600-pixel viewport, the browser asks: "Does (min-width: 1200px) match? No, moving on. Does (min-width: 800px) match? No, moving on. No qualifier. This image will occupy 100vw."
- For an 850-pixel viewport, the browser asks: "Does (min-width: 1200px) match? No, moving on. Does (min-width: 800px) match? Yes. This image will occupy 80vw."
- For a 1400-pixel viewport, the browser asks: "Does (min-width: 1200px) match? Yes. This image will occupy a space that is 1200px wide."

Now, if we had accidentally written that attribute the other way around, we'd have problems. An unqualified sizes value—one without a media query—is *always* going to match, at any viewport size. Once the browser encounters it, it throws the rest of the sizes attribute away:

```
sizes="100vw, (min-width: 800px) 80vw, (min-width:
1200px) 1200px"
```

- For a 600-pixel viewport, the browser says: "No qualifier. This image will occupy `100vw`."
- For an 850-pixel viewport, the browser says: "No qualifier. This image will occupy `100vw`."
- For a 1400-pixel viewport, the browser says: "No qualifier. This image will occupy `100vw`."

If we had put the (`min-width: 800px`) qualifier before (`min-width: 1200px`), we'd run into the same sort of problem. A viewport smaller than 800 pixels wouldn't qualify for the values scoped to either (`min-width: 800px`) or (`min-width: 1200px`), naturally. But a viewport wider than 1200 pixels is *also* going to match (`min-width: 800px`)—if we put that first, the browser stops there:

```
sizes="(min-width: 800px) 80vw, (min-width:
1200px) 1200px, 100vw"
```

- For a 600-pixel viewport, the browser asks: "Does (`min-width: 800px`) match? No, moving on. Does (`min-width: 1200px`) match? No, moving on. No qualifier. This image will occupy `100vw`."
- For an 850-pixel viewport, the browser asks: "Does (`min-width: 800px`) match? Yes. This image will occupy `80vw`."
- For a 1400-pixel viewport, the browser asks: "Does (`min-width: 800px`) match? Yes. This image will occupy `80vw`."

min-width **versus** max-width

When we use `min-width` media queries in a stylesheet, our unqualified styles represent our first breakpoint. We then override them with our smallest media query's styles, then override those with the next breakpoint up, and so on. Our unqualified styles apply on viewports *smaller* than the scope of our media queries.

We do the opposite when we use `max-width` media queries in a stylesheet: our first `max-width` media query is our first breakpoint, and we go upward from there. Our unqualified styles apply on viewports *larger* than the scope of our media queries.

Just like our CSS, `max-width` media queries in `sizes` will work the same way:

```
sizes="(max-width: 720px) 100vw, (max-width:
1250px) 80vw, 1500px"
```

- For a 600-pixel viewport, the browser asks: "Does (`max-width: 720px`) match? Yes. This image will occupy `100vw`."
- For an 850-pixel viewport, the browser asks: "Does (`max-width: 720px`) match? No, moving on. Does (`max-width: 1250px`) match? Yes. This image will occupy `80vw`."
- For a 1400-pixel viewport, the browser asks: "Does (`max-width: 720px`) match? No, moving on. Does (`max-width: 1250px`) match? No, moving on. No qualifier. This image will occupy `1500px`."

Now, I wouldn't fault you for asking why any of this is happening in an attribute at all. Markup feels like a strange place to encounter media queries, let alone write them—and presumably, the browser knows everything it needs to know about our layout on account of, you know, *rendering our layout*.

But at the time the browser initiates requests for images, it has no other information about the site—it may not have made requests for external stylesheets yet, or had a chance to apply them. Waiting until a page is fully rendered would mean introducing huge delays in requesting image sources—and once loaded, those images could then change the layout, causing a need for recalculation, and new requests for sources, and so on unto infinity.

In terms of `srcset`/`sizes`, we can safely say that the browser only knows a few things when it parses our markup and starts making external requests: the contents of that markup, the size of the viewport, and the pixel density of the display.

I wouldn't blame you for feeling a little wired after all that. These attributes pack an incredible amount of information into precious few characters. Once you learn the *rules* of `srcset` and `sizes`, though, you don't actually have to think much about how the browser makes decisions with those attributes. As a matter of fact, we *can't* know how the browser makes its decisions, given all this information. Believe it or not, that's by design—in fact, it might be the most exciting feature of responsive images.

The "explicitly vague" source-selection algorithm

You may have noticed that all of the responsive image solutions we've discussed only tangentially address the original problem we aimed to solve: serving bandwidth-appropriate assets to users.

From a syntax standpoint, telling the browser "use this source on a high-resolution display" or "here's some information, pick the right one for this viewport" is relatively easy—but knowing when a user *wants* high-resolution images is impossible. If I'm on a top-of-the-line MacBook but tethered to my phone's internet connection, using shaky airplane WiFi, or browsing the web by way of a metered connection, I might want to opt out of high-resolution image sources, regardless of my screen's capabilities.

These syntaxes can ensure that we're serving image assets more efficiently, but they can't do anything to address bandwidth concerns *directly*—and not for lack of trying. Members of the RICG and beyond spent a lot of time talking through how we could tailor assets to a user's bandwidth and what kind of syntax might make the most sense for that, revisiting the subject over and over. A server-side solution could give us an assumption based on the device, but a mobile device can be on anything from EDGE to WiFi.

We came up with what seemed like a perfectly sensible solution: a bandwidth media query. And after our initial excitement wore off, well—we came to hate our own idea.

We quickly realized we couldn't possibly ensure a consistent browsing experience for the user this way. Within the scope of a single project, sure—we could maintain a consistent bandwidth-based "breakpoint" for things like high-density images. But across the web, the browsing experience would be wildly inconsistent. Where *I* set that bandwidth breakpoint is different from where others might set it—a user could end up with high-resolution images on one site and low-resolution images on the next.

Worse still, we'd be making all of this óptional: one more thing to test, one more thing to go wrong, one more thing for us developers to keep in mind—or to forget. In cases where that media query was omitted, or set too high, the web would still *feel* broken to end users—slow and inconsiderate about bandwidth usage. On other pages, the web would *look* broken: unaware of the compromise being made on their behalf, a user would only know that they were seeing grainy images on their high-density display—something that wouldn't be the case on sites that set their bandwidth breakpoint a little higher.

There's a technical problem, too. Media queries feel like the right fit for bandwidth considerations, seeing as they're already designed to respond to client-side concerns—viewport height and width, device orientation, hardware features like ambient light level, and OS-level accessibility settings. But media queries are designed to respond to *changes* on the client side, and bandwidth can be unpredictable.

For example, when a user first lands on a page, they might qualify for our high-resolution images, then have their bandwidth drop off as they go through a tunnel. Now we have to send them low-resolution images, because that media query told the browser to listen for client-side bandwidth changes. As their connection speeds back up, we have to send them the high-resolution images again.

The only way to work around this would be to change the expected behavior of media queries from a guarantee ("if the viewport is smaller than 600 pixels, this will happen") to a potentiality ("if the viewport is smaller than 600 pixels, this may or may not happen"). That guarantee was the very thing that made media queries a natural fit for the art-direction use case: the source element that matches the media attribute we specify is the one that has to be used, full stop. Otherwise, we might end up with an image source that's inappropriate for the current layout.

But srcset is a syntax that's brand-new to the web, with no expected behaviors to redefine. So, the HTML5 specification defines srcset as a set of *candidates*. Any and all decisions about their use are left up to the browser, due to a critical feature of the selection algorithm encoded in the specification: once all the math has been done, and the sources and their descriptors have been sorted, the browser is free to do whatever it wants.

The syntaxes certainly *seem* declarative, but in practice, we're saying, "here is a source visually appropriate for devices with a `devicePixelRatio` of 2"—not "here is the source to use on devices with a `devicePixelRatio` of 2." The difference is slight in print, but huge in implication: nothing we include in `srcset` is a *command*, only a *candidate*.

That lack of explicit control can sound a little scary at face value, but `srcset`—using either the `devicePixelRatio` or `sizes` syntaxes—ultimately comes down to requesting one from a list of identical-looking sources. Because of that, there's very little room for an experience to seem *broken*, regardless of the decisions made by the browser.

By acting as a list of suggestions, `srcset` allows browsers to introduce user settings like "always give me low-res images"— something mobile Chrome's "data saver" mode does today. It paves the way for settings like "give me high-res images as bandwidth permits"—instead of instructing browsers to frantically respond to changes in bandwidth from one site to another, the browser can take an average across a given time frame or browsing session. Instead of developers drawing the line between delivering high- or low-resolution assets, with each of us landing in different places, those decisions can be made *by* the user, not *for* them.

It also means there's room for the browser to get creative—for example, in some browsers, an `img` or `source` marked up with the `srcset`/`sizes` syntax will never fire a request for a smaller source than the user already has in their browser's cache. After all, what would be the point in making a new request for a source with smaller dimensions, when the browser already has an identical-looking image that works for those viewport sizes? If the user scales their viewport up to the point where a new image is needed, that request will still get made—we want things to look seamless for them, after all, and upscaling a too-small image would look wrong.

The fact that we can't know for certain how srcset/sizes will behave to the end user? That's this use case's strongest feature.

MIXING AND MATCHING

There's one last aspect of the four responsive-image use cases I want to go over: combining them. We touched on it briefly early on, with picture using srcset's devicePixelRatio syntax on its source elements to provide both art direction *and* sources tailored to a user's display density.

Any and *all* of the four use cases can be used in concert:

```
<picture>
  <source
    media="(min-width: 1280px)"
    sizes="50vw"
    srcset="nomad-wide-200.webp 200w,
      nomad-wide-400.webp 400w,
      nomad-wide-800.webp 800w,
      nomad-wide-1200.webp 1200w,
      nomad-wide-1600.webp 1600w,
      nomad-wide-2000.webp 2000w"
    type="image/webp">
  <source
    sizes="(min-width: 640px) 60vw, 100vw"
    srcset="nomad-crop-200.webp 200w,
      nomad-crop-400.webp 400w,
      nomad-crop-800.webp 800w,
      nomad-crop-1200.webp 1200w,
      nomad-crop-1600.webp 1600w,
      nomad-crop-2000.webp 2000w"
    type="image/webp">
  <source
    media="(min-width: 1280px)"
    sizes="50vw"
    srcset="nomad-wide-200.jpg 200w,
      nomad-wide-400.jpg 400w,
```

```
        nomad-wide-800.jpg 800w,
        nomad-wide-1200.jpg 1200w,
        nomad-wide-1600.jpg 1800w,
        nomad-wide-2000.jpg 2000w">
  <img
    src="nomad-crop-400.jpg" alt="An orange-coated
shiba inu in the snow."
    sizes="(min-width: 640px) 60vw, 100vw"
    srcset="nomad-crop-200.jpg 200w,
        nomad-crop-400.jpg 400w,
        nomad-crop-800.jpg 800w,
        nomad-crop-1200.jpg 1200w,
        nomad-crop-1600.jpg 1600w,
        nomad-crop-2000.jpg 2000w">
</picture>
```

This monster of markup tells the browser:

- Using `type`, determine whether to use the `source` elements that reference WebP or standard JPEG images.
- Within each branch of that decision, use `media` as the selection criterion for each art-directed `source`.
- Once the final `source` has been selected, choose from a list of candidate sources inside the `srcset` attribute, with `sizes` describing the space the image will occupy within that range of viewport sizes.
- If none of the `source` elements apply due to the current viewport size and/or browser's WebP support, render the inner `img` as-is, using `srcset`/`sizes`.
- If none of the responsive-image markup patterns are supported by the user's browser, render the `src` of the inner `img` element.
- If the user is navigating by way of assistive technologies, narrate "an orange-coated shiba inu in the snow."

Now, I can say with some certainty that you'll never need to do this—I know I've never even come *close*. `srcset`/`sizes` on a single `img` is generally all I need, with only the occasional `picture` interlude.

I say all this to point out how much has changed in just a few short years: from a single method of showing a single image source, with no opportunity to apply any conditional logic, to an *incredible* number of mix-and-match options for smarter asset delivery, with all of the performance, accessibility, and reliability of our old friend `img`.

With so many options at our disposal—and with even the most common single use case being a little unintuitive—I wouldn't blame you for feeling a bit rattled. I certainly was, seeing the code snippet above for the very first time: not only would I be stuck *using* all of this in my day-to-day work, but I would know exactly whom to blame for such a sprawling syntax: me.

HOW I LEARNED TO STOP WORRYING AND LOVE RESPONSIVE IMAGES

I've mentioned a few times that some of these syntaxes aren't for *us*, so much as they're for computers. They're terse by necessity—that much was apparent early on in the specification process. Anything we might have done to make these syntaxes a little less dense—and more easily parsed by us humans—could have made them more complex for a browser to parse. Adding complexity to a parser translates to more potential for bugs, or for unintentional differences in behavior from one browser to another.

But as much as that density feels like a syntactical weakness when we're rooting through all this markup by hand, it reveals itself to be a strength in practice: a syntax more easily read by machines is a syntax more easily *written* by them.

Creating alternate cuts of an image, outside of manual art direction, is a task that content management systems (CMS) have been handling for us since time immemorial—you'd be hard-pressed to find a mainstream CMS that doesn't offer something in the way of "thumbnails" generated from uploaded images, whether natively or via plugin. It isn't much of a stretch to imagine that pattern extended just a little further, allowing the CMS to generate all of the images we could want to populate a `srcset` attribute, and—knowing all of the sizes it was told to generate—the syntax to match.

WordPress was one of the earliest adopters of native responsive-images markup, starting in version 4.4, and it does exactly that:

> *A new default intermediate size,* `medium_large`*, has been added to better take advantage of responsive image support. The new size is 768px wide by default, with no height limit, and can be used like any other size available in WordPress. As it is a standard size, it will only be generated when new images are uploaded or sizes are regenerated with third party plugins.*

Whether via CMS, a task runner like Grunt or Gulp, or even a third-party service like Cloudinary, `srcset` is a relatively simple case for automation.

`sizes` is a little harder. Since it should refer to the *displayed* size of the image, it doesn't lend itself well to defaults.

Now, this doesn't mean `sizes` doesn't have a default *behavior.* If that attribute is left empty, or omitted altogether, the browser will assume a `sizes` value of `100vw`, in order to err on the side of excessively large images rather than images that could appear distorted. This doesn't *prevent* potential visual issues, though: by telling the browser than an image is meant to occupy 100 percent of the available viewport width, the browser will attempt to use it as the image's natural width. Unless acted on by CSS—using a maximum `width` on either the `img` or its container—that image could be scaled beyond its source's maximum size.

This led to a default `sizes` attribute in the Word-Press implementation:

```
(max-width: {{image-width}}px) 100vw, {{image-
    width}}px
```

In other words: "`100vw`, up to a viewport width equal to the width of the uploaded image; beyond that, a fixed width equal to the image's natural width." This ensures that the behavior of the `img` more or less matches the behavior of an `img` with a `src` pointing at the uploaded image. And, of course, the WordPress team provided an API hook that allows authors to supply their own `sizes` attributes within their templates.

That would still mean *writing* that attribute by hand, but tools have popped up to abstract that away, and with an efficiency we could never match by hand: the `RespImageLint project`, for example, provides you with a bookmarklet that vets your `sizes` attributes for accuracy and efficiency, and provides suggestions for potential improvements. Even as steeped as I am in this topic, I never leave home without it.

On a personal site, I recently encountered the following situation: I had written, manually, what I thought to be a perfectly respectable `sizes` attribute, based on a little back-of-napkin math, performed by my perfectly average human brain:

```
(min-width: 1480px) 935px, (min-width: 800px) 64vw,
  98vw
```

Close enough, I figured. A pass through RespImgLint, however, resulted in the following:

```
(min-width: 1560px) calc(-1.25vw + 358px), (min-
  width: 760px) calc(21.03vw + 14px), (min-width:
  500px) 47.5vw, 97.22vw
```

That's math I could never have hoped to reason through, considering the degree to which I struggle when it comes time to calculate a tip. But by simulating the resizing of a browser window and calculating the precise space each `img` element occupies in a page's layout at each viewport size, RespImageLint suggests an incredibly tailored `sizes` attribute—which, in terms of asset delivery, would no doubt be just a hair more efficient than mine. And with countless users loading countless pages, a kilobyte here or there can certainly add up.

But that's not the entire appeal for me. See, by not writing these attributes by hand—by using a tool like RespImgLint to generate a hyper-optimized `sizes` value, plus a task runner or CMS to generate alternate image cuts and a corresponding `srcset` value, and with a template engine to bind it all together for me—I barely have to think about responsive images at all these days.

They're no less important, of course. I still get to provide users with an experience that feels tailored, in a completely invisible way—they'll never know what responsive-image use cases I sought to address for them, or how I went about doing it. Nothing will look any different from any other site they've encountered over the years: their images will look as sharp as their display (and their eyes) will allow. Those images will be sized the way our layouts dictate—the way users have come to expect from a well-crafted website.

But our sites will feel faster. And as these techniques propagate more and more, the web *itself* will feel faster, with no cost to the people using it—no drawbacks, no compromises, no hacks, and no grainy images.

CONCLUSION

In a way, this book was to be my images-on-the-web swan song. The RICG's work on images has long since concluded, its members scattering to work on browsers and CDNs and CMSes, to write guides and tutorials, to give talks and lead workshops. Together, they're pushing the web toward something better, faster, and more inclusive, whether they're building the tools or teaching others how to use them.

I had this conclusion all mapped out in my head, because the contents of it were, sadly, already second nature. I was going to wrap things up the way I've concluded so many talks and blog posts about how images work on the web: with a plea. Try harder; do better. Websites keep getting larger, month after month, and image transfers are still responsible for most of the damage. The web is becoming more exclusive—something for the few, for those with the same browsing privilege as the people building it. We developers are *severing* peoples' connections to the web, rather than helping to build them. I'd sound the call-to-arms: we have to try harder. We have the tools; we need to use them. We can do better. We *have* to do better. Can't you see that we're *losing*?

But, in reviewing statistics from HTTP Archive, I saw something I've never seen before: during the course of 2018, the median image transfer size has been declining month to month.

We *are* doing better.

The momentum, finally, might just be on our side, thanks to countless hours of work by countless developers, designers, educators, and writers—and thanks to you. You're someone who believes that anything worth doing is worth doing well. You're someone who doesn't take anything for granted—not even a topic as "simple" as putting images on the web.

I wrote this book for you. But you—you're writing this ending for me.

ACKNOWLEDGMENTS

I can't believe they let me do this *again*.

The "they" in question is, of course, the team at A Book Apart. They're a "they" of incredible talent, patience, and—apart from *me*, the one glaring blemish on their otherwise impeccable record—taste in authors. Katel, Jeffrey, and Jason: thank you so, so much for this opportunity, and for so many others.

Lisa Maria Martin, my editor: thank you for so diligently holding me to account for deadlines. Lisa Maria Martin, my girlfriend: thank you for encouraging me to blow off those deadlines every once in a while. As always, and as in all things: I couldn't do it without you.

Finally, to the RICG:

To Eric Portis, my technical editor, whose writing on the subject of responsive images has always far eclipsed my own.

To Yoav Weiss and Marcos Caceres, who did all the heavy lifting from the very start.

To every one of you—every member of the nebulous, pirate-radio web standards group who managed to change the way the web is built through sheer determination.

And to you, reader, for fighting the good fight.

Thank you.

RESOURCES

Now what? Well, there are a couple pages you can turn to for the next step in your image-performance choose-your-own-adventure story.

If you want to dig even further into the topic of image formats, I've got good news: even with as much as we've covered here, we're still just *barely* scratching the surface. *High-Performance Images*—which counts a number of RICG members in its list of authors—will take you even further into the realm of encodings, algorithms, and quirks. Jeremy Wagner's *The WebP Manual* is absolutely required reading.

If you can't get enough of responsive images, well, who could blame you? Eric Portis, who was kind enough to provide technical editing for this book, is a prolific writer on the subject himself:

- "Responsive Images in Practice"
- "Srcset and Sizes"
- "Responsive Images Done Right"

It probably goes without saying, but Scott Jehl's *Responsible Responsive Web Design* and Ethan Marcotte's *Responsive Design: Patterns & Principles* are both absolutely essential reads, on the topic of images and so much more.

REFERENCES

Shortened URLs are numbered sequentially; the related long URLs are listed below for reference.

Introduction

00-01 https://www.httparchive.org/reports/page-weight?start=2017_04_0 1&end=latest

00-02 http://radar.oreilly.com/2014/01/web-performance-is-user-experience.html

00-03 http://www.pewinternet.org/fact-sheet/mobile/

00-04 http://www.pewinternet.org/2015/04/01/us-smartphone-use-in-2015/

00-05 https://www.ericsson.com/assets/local/mobility-report/documents/2016/ ericsson-mobility-report-feb-2016-interim.pdf

Chapter 1

01-01 https://bugs.chromium.org/p/chromium/issues/detail?id=791658

01-02 https://en.wikipedia.org/wiki/Discrete_cosine_transform

01-03 https://www.toptal.com/developers/sorting-algorithms

01-04 https://github.com/kornelski/dssim

01-05 https://cloudinary.com/blog/progressive_jpegs_and_green_martians

Chapter 2

02-01 https://andydavies.me/blog/2013/10/22/how-the-browser-pre-loader-makes-pages-load-faster/

02-02 https://developer.mozilla.org/en-US/docs/Web/HTTP/Basics_of_HTTP/ MIME_types

02-03 https://make.wordpress.org/core/2015/11/10/responsive-images-in-wordpress-4-4/

02-04 https://github.com/ausi/ResplmageLint

Conclusion

03-01 https://www.httparchive.org/reports/page-weight?start=2018_01_01&en d=latest#bytesImg

Resources

04-01 http://shop.oreilly.com/product/0636920039730.do

04-02 https://www.smashingmagazine.com/ebooks/the-webp-manual/

04-03 https://alistapart.com/article/responsive-images-in-practice

04-04 https://ericportis.com/posts/2014/srcset-sizes/

04-05 https://www.smashingmagazine.com/2014/05/responsive-images-done-right-guide-picture-srcset/

04-06 https://abookapart.com/products/responsible-responsive-design

04-07 https://abookapart.com/products/responsive-design-patterns-principles

INDEX

S

scripting 7-8
source-selection algorithm 52-54
SVG (Scalable Vector Graphics) 6-9

T

tailoring assets 31-35
task runners 58
transparency 14

V

vector formats 6-10
very good boy (Zero the dog) 21
video source files 17

W

W3C 34
Web Hypertext Application
       Technology Working Group
       (WHATWG) 35
WebP 29, 39-40

Z

ZIP 18

ABOUT A BOOK APART

We cover the emerging and essential topics in web design and development with style, clarity, and above all, brevity—because working designer-developers can't afford to waste time.

COLOPHON

The text is set in FF Yoga and its companion, FF Yoga Sans, both by Xavier Dupré. Headlines and cover are set in Titling Gothic by David Berlow.

ABOUT THE AUTHOR

Mat "Wilto" Marquis is an amateur boxer, aspiring chef, half-way decent carpenter, and passable antique British motorcycle mechanic—when not making fast, accessible, responsive websites. He keeps busy.

As chair of the Responsive Issues Community Group, Mat spearheaded the effort to bring native responsive image solutions to the HTML5 specification, later going on to facilitate browser implementations and oversee the addition of native responsive image techniques to major CMSes. He has spoken at An Event Apart, edited for *A List Apart,* and published *Java-Script for Web Designers* with A Book Apart, completing what he describes as "like an EGOT, but for putting semicolons in the right places."